DATE DUE			

All by Herself

All by

HARCOURT, INC.

San Diego   New York   London

POEMS BY

ANN WHITFORD PAUL

Herself

*14 Girls Who
Made a Difference*

ILLUSTRATED BY

MICHAEL STEIRNAGLE

Library of Congress Cataloging-in-Publication Data
Paul, Ann Whitford.
All by herself/Ann Whitford Paul; illustrated by Michael Steirnagle. — 1st ed.
p. cm.
Summary: Poems recount the stories of fourteen girls, some of whom later
became famous, who performed acts of daring, determination, and heroic
courage at a young age.
1. Girls — Biography — Juvenile poetry. 2. Children's poetry, American.
[1. Women heroes — Poetry. 2. Courage — Poetry. 3. American poetry.
4. Girls — Biography — Poetry.] I. Steirnagle, Michael, ill. II. Title.
PS3566.A826148A75 1999
811'.54 — dc21   97-5871
ISBN 0-15-201477-2

K J I H G F

Printed in Hong Kong

ACKNOWLEDGMENTS
Thanks to all the librarians across the country who so willingly answered
my many queries. Thanks also to the Huntington Library in San Marino, California,
for allowing me access to its wonderful collection, and especially to Paul Zall,
who always knew how to point me to the right book

In memory of
Myra Cohn Livingston,
with me every poem I write
—A. W. P.

For my son, Matthew, and
my daughter, Stacy
—M. S.

Amelia Earhart

While other girls wore skirts and pinafores,
Amelia much preferred to dress in bloomers.
She hated playing with dolls and sipping tea.
Amelia loved to climb and swing from trees.
At seven she came up with an idea.
"Let's build a roller coaster in the yard.
Come on," she begged her sister. "It's not hard."

They started on the project right away
and dragged long planks out from the cellar
to the tool shed—eight feet tall.
The perfect size!
(And hidden far away from parents' eyes!)
Amelia climbed the roof and started banging nails
to make each track stay in its place.
A wooden crate would be the cart to race.

She slathered up the boards with lots of lard.
Amelia was the first to try the ride.
Down she zipped!
                    A whiz!
                              A blur!
                                        A flash!
Suddenly, she flipped.
There was a crash.
The roller coaster broke apart.
Amelia jumped right up without a bit of crying
and happily proclaimed,
"It's just like flying!"

Mary Jane McLeod

She went with Mama to her work,
washing, ironing white folks' clothes.
Their girls invited her to come inside their playhouse,
and have some fun with dolls.
But Mary Jane saw a book.
She picked it up to have a look.
　　　They laughed. "Put that down!
　　　You don't know how to read."
They spoke the truth.
All southern schools were closed to her.
One day a woman came to town to open a place
to teach young students of any race.
Mary Jane asked her parents, "Can I go?
You need me picking cotton, I know,
　　　but someone in our family
　　　has to learn to read."
They understood how much this meant
and so they gladly gave their blessing.
She had to walk alone every day
on dusty roads, five miles each way.
Her teacher had dark skin, too.
She told her students what to do.
　　　"Pay attention. Study hard
　　　and soon you'll read."
Sometimes it rained and harsh winds blew,
but Mary Jane didn't miss a day.
She studied long into the night,
a candle flame her only light.
She worked and struggled at that school,
so she would not grow up a fool,
　　　so people couldn't laugh at her.
　　　She learned to read!

Violet Sheehy

High heat met dry timber! Fire out of control!
A dark heavy smoke surged into the sky.
Violet shuddered. She started to cry and raced to get Mother.
"The danger is great! We have to leave home!
There's no time to wait!"
The wind howled. It gusted.
She begged Mother, "Come!"
and picked up the baby and started to run.
But Mother just walked,
bewildered and stunned by her fear
for the children she had in tow.
They'd never escape if she kept on so slow.
The young girl dashed back.
"Mother! Run fast!
The fire's a monster! See how it speeds!
Don't let it catch us! Follow my lead!"
Mrs. Sheehy moved faster, but in a short while—
before they had barely traveled a mile—
she faltered and wearily sank to the ground.
The heat seared. The smoke blinded, but Violet rushed back.
"Why are you stopping? The sky is all black!"
She grasped Mother's arm. "No! You can't stay!"
She yanked Mother up and pulled her away.
At last they reached town.
Sparks swirled! Cinders sprayed!
Every church, every store was swallowed in flame.
All around people shouted, "Jump on the train!"
Violet's family, frightened and dazed,
stumbled onto the train that churned through the blaze.

Hundreds of people perished that day,
but Violet's strength kept her family alive.
Her brother and sisters and mother survived,
although hardly a tree was uncharred in the wood.
Not one single house in the town still stood.

Rachel Carson

When Rachel was a child,
she hiked alone around her farm
and learned the names of flowers growing wild
and bugs and birds and trees.

When Rachel was a child,
after chores of milking cows
and making cheese, collecting eggs,
she read.
Her fondness was for nature books.
Sometimes she made up stories in her head
and wrote them down.

When she was only ten,
she overcame her shyness and,
addressing carefully,
sent one story to a magazine.
So pleased to see her words in print,
she knew what she would do
when she was not a child—
she'd write about the flowers
bugs and birds and trees
and all things growing wild.

Sacajawea

Long years ago a girl embarked
with two explorers, Lewis and Clark,
to learn about uncharted land.
She crossed the plains
and climbed gigantic mountains,
forged the rivers snaking through the woods.
She circled lakes.
With her baby on her back,
alert for bear and lion tracks,
she showed them shortcuts through the hills.
When men fell sick, she nursed the ill.
She introduced them to wild plants,
when all the men were ignorant of what was food.
And when they met her kin, she said,
"Feel no threat," in their own native tongue.
"Come trade your horses, share your meat."
They aided Lewis and Clark.
                    So many hills to climb...
traveling on for two years' time,
trudging, tramping day by day,
wending, winding on her way,
with every dauntless step she took,
she walked into our history books.

Ida Lewis

From the lighthouse
Ida saw
the clouds turn black and threatening,
and cold gray waves crash roughly down.
Four brash young men stepped in a boat,
then raised the sails and hoisted off—
left Newport for the open seas.

From the lighthouse
Ida watched
one man scale the narrow mast.
The boat heaved wildly side to side.
Higher, higher up he climbed.
The mast began to tilt.
It swayed and drenched him in the icy water.

In the lighthouse
Ida gasped.
He lost his grip!
The boat capsized and pitched them all into the ocean.
Frantically, they clutched the hull,
their shouting silenced by the storm.

From the lighthouse
Ida dashed
and quickly leaped into her boat.
She stabbed her oars through raging swells.
Her small skiff pitched. Her small skiff plunged.
Her arms grew weak and stiff,
but still she rowed until she reached their side.
Jabbing out her wooden oar,
she dragged them from the frigid seas,
then, soaked and spent, she turned the boat and...
to the lighthouse
Ida rowed.

Harriet Hanson

At five A.M. her work began,
changing bobbins—filled for empty.
She drudged twelve hours through each day,
six days a week for paltry pay—
until the bosses cut all wages.

In factories around the town rose loud complaints.
"This isn't right," the mill girls shouted. "We will fight!"
Some risked their jobs, went out on strike,
and marched as one down the street.
Arm in arm,
they sang their song.

Harriet's friends were scared.
They argued long.
Their parents counted on their earnings.
Should they stay or turn-out, too?
The strikers were about to pass.
"I'm tired of talk!" she spoke at last.
"I don't care what you might do!
I'll go alone."

Harriet joined the throng,
but then she saw—
a surging swirl
of fellow workers follow *her*!

Wilma Rudolph

One leg was bent; her foot turned in.
She had to wear a heavy brace
and an ugly, hateful shoe.
Each pace, each step, she scraped and clunked.
Kids gathered close to stare at her
and taunt and tease.
Slowly,
Wilma hobbled off.
She found a secret place,
unbuckled the brace, untied the shoe,
then yanked them off.
Every day she practiced walking.
How it hurt to hold her leg the normal way!
At first Wilma stumbled.
She dragged her foot.
Step, slow step…
slow lurching steps…
until she learned to walk!
Faster! Faster!
Wilma began
        to run.
            She ran
                and ran
                    and ran.

Wanda Gág

When Father died, the neighbors told her,
"Quit school, Wanda. Go to work."
With seven children's mouths to fill,
her mother sorely needed help,
for she was frail and gravely ill.

No. Wanda wouldn't quit.
She stayed in school,
then after class she dusted, swept,
and cooked a brothy stew.
She patched and mended piles of clothes,
washed and did the ironing, too.

Later while the whole house slept,
though weary,
Wanda dipped her pen in ink,
and drew pictures she could sell to magazines.
Her postcards, place cards,
and small bookmarks all sold well,
as did her cards for holidays.
She kept a record of each sale
and every night toiled late again.
She finished school—her siblings, too!—
supported by her artist's pen.

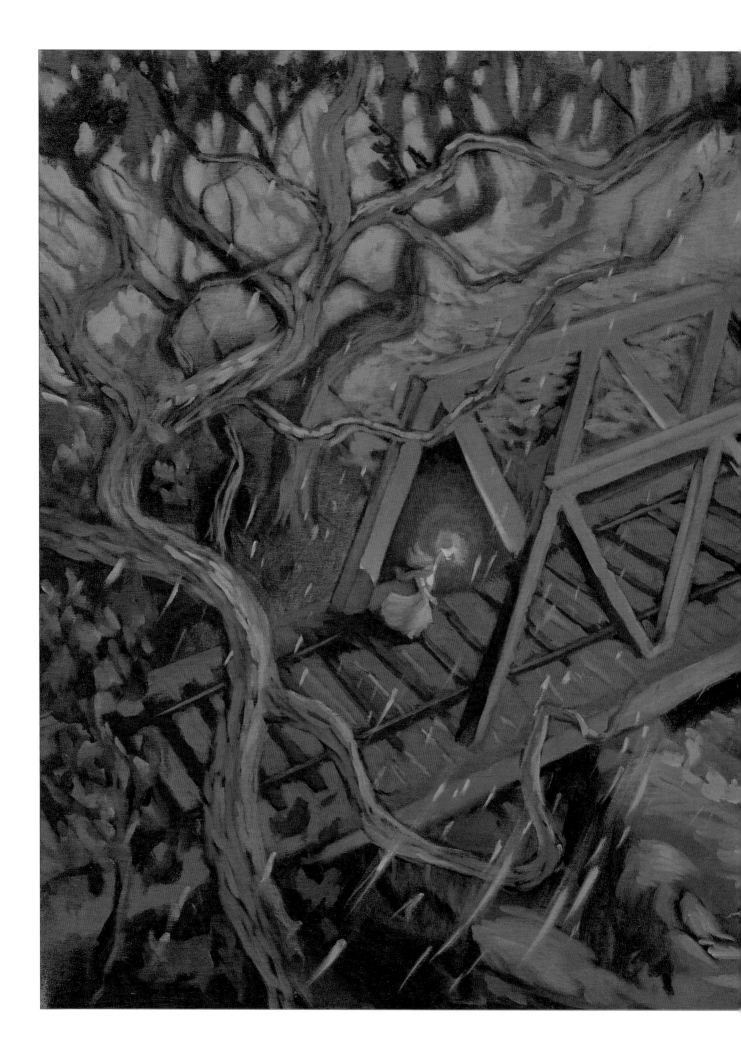

Kate Shelley

Lightning ripped apart the sky. Thunder pounded loud,
hammering relentlessly. Rain pelted from the clouds.
Kate Shelley trembled—Mother, too—at the raging storm.
They moved in closer to their hearth,
dry and safe and warm.
Then on the tracks nearby their home,
men rode a service train to check the rails
for damage caused by so much pouring rain.
Kate heard its bell toll once, twice, and then a roar of sound,
as if the thunder rumbled in the belly of the ground.
Kate grabbed her lantern.
Mother begged her, "Stay!" but Kate dashed out.
The bridge was smashed! The train had crashed!
Two men clung desperately to trees.
Kate started into town for help.
The path was overgrown—she tripped and tumbled down.
Kate stood again and ran
until she reached Des Moines' wide river.
The water lapped the railroad bridge.
Her lantern's small flame quivered. Then it died!
Kate strained to see the ties placed far apart,
stooped down to her knees, and groped on through the dark.
Jabbed by splinters, ripped by nails,
she crawled along the planks—across a span, five hundred feet.
At last she reached the bank.
Cold and wet seeped to her bones,
yet still she ran—raced fast!—to town.
The people there were horrified.
They gasped and hurried with her to the train.
Though nearly drained of hope,
the men were pulled to safety with a long and looping rope.
Kate Shelley didn't wait for thanks,
but trudged on through the storm,
back to Mother, back to home,
dry and safe and warm.

Pocahontas

Young daughter of a native chief,
the thoughtful Pocahontas hid behind a tree,
and watched the pale-skinned men,
heeding everything they did—
pounding fence posts, building forts.
Then she raced home to tell of all that she had seen.
Her kinsmen, frightened by her news,
quickly called a powwow
and pondered what to do.
She overheard their plan to kill and force the colonists away,
but kept her silence well until
her people captured Captain Smith.
They brought him to the chief—bedecked in fur,
a long and regal robe,
with ropes of pearls about his neck.

Another powwow was begun.
Each sage, each shaman argued loud.
Somberly, the chief decreed, "The prisoner must die!"
A crowd surrounded Captain Smith.
They dragged him down, and raised their deadly clubs.
Pocahontas flung herself upon his head.
One blow: her blood would flow, not his.
Her father ordered, "Halt!"
He let the captain go back home again.

Soon afterward a fire blazed, a dreadful glow,
destroying all the settlers' food.
Pocahontas felt their grief.
She gave them deer meat, turkey, corn.
She alone brought them relief.
Many owed their lives to her—
young daughter of a native chief.

Maria Mitchell

With her father, each clear night,
Maria watched the dome of sky,
studying with a careful eye,
entranced by every cosmic sight.
He let her use his telescope,
so she could see the lights out far—
the color, gleam of every star.
She kept a journal, where she wrote
her observations down.
One day,
a captain of a sailing ship
brought his sea clock to be fixed.
"I'm sorry, Father's gone away
for several days." The look on his face
spoke clearly. "Miss, I cannot wait."
Maria didn't hesitate.
"I'll fix it in my father's place.
I've watched him well. I know
the way to mend this clock. You'll see.
I'll do it right, so out at sea
you'll keep your bearings as you go."
The captain gazed at her askance,
worried, staring at her curls.
"You're scarce fourteen! You're but a girl!"
Should he, dare he, take a chance?
He did.
And all alone that night
Maria measured stars, drew lines,
made adjustments, checked the times,
and by the early morning light,
his clock worked smoothly as before.
The captain sailed that very day.
Maria waved. He'd find the way,
because of her, back safe to shore.

Golda Mabovitch

Her family left the town of Pinsk,
fled hunger and religious strife,
searching for a better life.
Milwaukee was her newfound home —
There her dad could work and earn,
and even girls could go to learn
in schools that didn't cost one cent,
except for books — a little fee.
But some friends lived in poverty
and buying books was out of reach.
Though just a student in fourth grade,
Golda ran a book crusade.
She painted posters and sent out mail.
She found a meeting hall to use for free.
That wasn't all!
After other girls sang songs and recited poems,
came Golda's part.
The girl from Pinsk spoke from her heart —
words not written in advance —
urging everyone to share their extra change
to care for those less fortunate.
The people listened and were stirred.
When she finished, Golda heard
the clink of coins to help the poor.
Her simple words were all it took
for every child to own a book.

Frances Ward

For months and months her wagon train
inched through sunshine, hail, and rain.
Her feet were blistered
from walking...walking...every day.
Sometimes she wandered far astray
to gather pungent chips for fires.
Frances pitched the tent and helped to cook
and often went to scrub the dirty clothes in streams.
Her hands grew chapped and sore,
but every day there were more chores
and endless walking...walking....

One noon a horse,
tied to a tree trunk,
snapped his rope and trotted free.
Frances gave chase. She grabbed his mane.
He dragged her roughly past the prickly shrubs
and raced wind-fast.
"I'll not let go!" she cried,
and flung herself up on his back.
She whacked his neck—a stinging smack.
He shied. He kicked.
He bucked and snorted, reared and galloped on.
She feared he'd race until the dawn.

At last he tired and slowed.
Frances stroked his sweaty mane
and rode him back, now calm and tame.
Yet no one cheered for her.
Most people laughed and teased her, too, said,
"What a reckless thing to do! You should have been a boy!"
But she ignored each taunt and call,
dismounted, stood pine-straight and tall,
and went on walking...walking....

Afterword

Each by herself has acted strong.
This book is short,
but could be long.
Many girls have done the same,
but there's not room
for every name.

About the Girls

Amelia Earhart built her roller coaster in 1904. When she grew up, she became a pilot and was the first woman to fly alone across the Atlantic  Ocean. At the age of thirty-nine, she disappeared with her plane on a flight across the Pacific Ocean.

 *Mary Jane McLeod* was about ten years old when she first attended school. She worked all her life to improve education for African Americans, and using her married name, Mary McLeod Bethune, she founded a school, known today as Bethune-Cookman College, in Daytona Beach, Florida.

Violet Sheehy was twelve years old on Saturday, September 1, 1894, when fire struck the town of Hinckley, Minnesota. Because lumber companies  often used controlled fires to clear the cut-forest land of stumps, the townspeople did not realize their danger until it was too late. Many years passed before Violet and other survivors wrote down their memories of that frightening day.

 In 1918 *Rachel Carson* received a ten-dollar prize for the publication of her story "A Battle in the Clouds" in *St. Nicholas* magazine. When she grew up, she wrote books that awakened people to the joys of the natural world and to the threats industry poses to plants and wildlife. She is called the mother of the modern ecology movement.

Sacajawea was about sixteen years old when, in 1805, she and her husband and new baby son set out with the Lewis and Clark expedition.  There is much speculation about her life afterward, but little is known for sure. Some say she died young; others say she lived a long time.

About the Girls (continued)

Ida Lewis was just sixteen years old when she saved four young men off the coast of Newport, Rhode Island, in 1858. It was the first of many such rescues for Ida, who, after her father died, took over as keeper of the Lime Rock Lighthouse.

Born prematurely, *Wilma Rudolph* suffered many serious childhood illnesses, which weakened her and caused one foot to turn in. At age twenty, she finished first in the 100-meter dash in the 1960 Olympics. She also won the 200-meter dash and ran with the victorious 400-meter relay team, making her the first American woman to win three gold medals in track and field at a single Olympics.

In October 1836 eleven-year-old *Harriet Hanson* was one of many young girls employed in the fabric mills of Lowell, Massachusetts. Although the other girls who labored in Harriet's workroom followed her lead and joined the general strike, or turn-out, as it was called, working conditions did not improve. Eventually Harriet married, and after her husband died, she supported herself and her children by writing and by renting out rooms. She was active in the movement to give women the right to vote.

In 1908 fifteen-year-old *Wanda Gág* started keeping the journal that described these events. She continued working in art all of her life, exhibiting at galleries, and writing and illustrating children's books, including the popular *Millions of Cats*.

For her heroism on July 6, 1881, fifteen-year-old *Kate Shelley* received a gold medal from the state of Iowa. As an adult she worked as a railroad station agent, selling tickets and billing freight. Whenever she rode a train, the railroad men honored her by making a special stop to let her off at her house.

Pocahontas was about twelve years old when, according to writings of Captain John Smith, she stopped his execution in 1607. From that day forth, Pocahontas was a good friend to him and the settlers of Jamestown, Virginia, giving them food, translating for them, and teaching them about their new land. Eventually, she married an English settler named John Rolfe. They had one son. Pocahontas died soon afterward, on a visit to England.

In 1832 *Maria* (pronounced mah-*rye*-a) *Mitchell* repaired the captain's sea clock (or chronometer) so he could steer his ship by the stars. Years later she looked through her telescope and saw a comet no one else had ever seen. The king of Denmark awarded her a gold medal for her discovery. Although largely self-educated, Maria taught for many years as a professor of astronomy at Vassar College in Poughkeepsie, New York.

In 1909 *Golda Mabovitch*, an immigrant from the town of Pinsk in Russia, made her first plea for money to help needy people. In adulthood, when she was known as Golda Meir, she raised funds for the new Jewish state of Israel, and in 1969 she became its prime minister.

Many girls and boys, women and men, migrated in wagon trains across the Great Plains to settle along the West Coast. *Frances Ward* was in her late teens in 1853 when she and her family left their home in the Midwest and traveled more than two thousand miles. Her mother kept a journal of their long trip and described this incident. The Ward family settled in California.

Select Bibliography

Anderson, Antone A., and Clara Anderson McDermott, editors. *The Hinckley Fire: Stories from the Hinckley Fire Survivors*. New York: Comet Press Books, 1954.

Brewerton, George D. *Ida Lewis: The Heroine of Lime Rock*. Newport, R. I.: A. J. Ward, 1896.

Bushman, Claudia L. *A Good Poor Man's Wife: Being a Chronicle of Harriet Hanson Robinson and Her Family in Nineteenth-Century New England*. Hanover, N. H.: University Press of New England, 1981.

Embree, Edwin R. *Against the Odds*. New York: The Viking Press, 1944.

Gág, Wanda. *Growing Pains: Diaries and Drawings for the Years 1908–1917*. New York: Coward-McCann, 1940.

Howard, Harold P. *Sacajawea*. Norman: University of Oklahoma Press, 1971.

James, Edward T., editor. *Notable American Women 1607–1950: A Biographical Dictionary*. Cambridge, Mass.: The Belknap Press of Harvard University Press, 1971.

McCay, Mary A. *Rachel Carson*. New York: Twayne Publishers, 1993.

Meir, Golda. *My Life*. New York: G. P. Putnam's Sons, 1975.

Morrissey, Muriel Earhart. *Courage Is the Price: The Biography of Amelia Earhart*. Witchita, Kans.: McCormick-Armstrong Publishing Division, 1963.

Mossiker, Frances. *Pocahontas*. New York: Alfred A. Knopf, 1976.

Rudolph, Wilma, and Martin Ralbovsky, editorial associate. *Wilma*. New York: New American Library, 1977.

Swisher, J. A. "Kate Shelley." *The Palimpsest* (February 1925). State Historical Society of Iowa.

Ward, Harriet Sherril. *Prairie Schooner Lady*. Edited by Ward G. DeWitt and Florence Stark DeWitt. Los Angeles: Westernlore Press, 1959.

Wright, Helen. *Sweeper in the Sky: The Life of Maria Mitchell, First Woman Astronomer in America*. New York: The Macmillan Publishing Company, 1949.

The illustrations in this book were done in oils on canvas.

The display type was set in Florens Flourished.

The text type was set in Cochin.

Color separations by Bright Arts Ltd., Hong Kong

Printed by South China Printing Company, Ltd., Hong Kong

This book was printed on totally chlorine-free Nymolla Matte Art paper.

Production supervision by Stanley Redfern and Ginger Boyer

Designed by Linda Lockowitz